MW01093741

# First Steps to Cash

By
David Neagle

# COPYRIGHT

# TABLE OF CONTENTS

INTRODUCTION............................................................ 1

THE BACK STORY....................................................... 3

FINANCIAL FREEDOM.............................................. 8

BRINGING MONEY INTO YOUR LIFE ...................15

WHY YOU NEED THE MONEY...............................25

WHAT'S HOLDING YOU BACK..............................32

THE LAW OF POLARITY..........................................37

THE EXCUSE................................................................51

MONEY, THE ROOT OF SO MUCH GOOD............58

STRUGGLING TO SUCCESS....................................64

THE FOUR STEPS TO CASH ON YOUR
JOURNEY TO ABUNDANCE ....................................72

MESSAGE FROM DAVID...........................................73

ABOUT THE AUTHOR ..............................................75

## DAVID SPEAKS

I want to personally thank you for making the decision to significantly up-level your life and for purchasing my eBook!

I'm delighted to give you private access to 3 powerful bonuses (worth over $300!) not available anywhere on our website!

**Check the link to access your**

# Manifest Your Millions Within

**eBook Series Gifts.**
**(http://www.davidneagle.com/transform/kindlebook)**

I encourage you to download these **3 bonuses** today and implement what you learn. Remember, **"Through decision and action, anything is possible!"**

-David Neagle

\*\*\*\*\*\*\*\*\*\*\*\*\*\*\*\*

**MORE KINDLE BOOKS FROM DAVID NEAGLE**

When you're finished reading this book, download the other volumes of the Manifest Your Millions

Within series by David Neagle available on Amazon Kindle.

## The Mental Money Game
(http://www.amazon.com/Mental-Manifest-Millions-Within-ebook/dp/B0081IOOL4)

## The Neagle Code
(http://www.amazon.com/Neagle-Manifest-Millions-Within-ebook/dp/B0081KQ2AI)

## Mastering the Massive Cash Injection
(http://www.amazon.com/Mastering-Injection-Manifest-Millions-ebook/dp/B0081KQ1JK)

## The 7 Mental Money Secrets of Millionaire Entrepreneurs
(http://www.amazon.com/Millionaire-Entrepreneurs-Manifest-Millions-ebook/dp/B0081IOOGY)

# INTRODUCTION

The idea of making more money and having the ability to make more money is a very personal journey for you, one that you should treat with great respect. You're going to be very pleasantly surprised and excited to be going on this journey yourself. You should be.

First, we will concentrate on "The Fast Cash Formula." You will learn about systematic ways to bring fast cash into your business and your life. You don't even have to have a business right now. This is simple stuff. These are concepts you apply no matter where you are or what you're doing. Wherever you are now, these steps will help you move onto the next level.

Our second focus will be on specifically what's holding you back. You will learn how to recognize those behaviors that detract from your good. If choosing lack over abundance is prevalent in your life, you will learn to see what it looks like and why you're doing it, from a self-sabotage standpoint.

Self-sabotage may be a harsh term. We view it sometimes as if we're really doing something to hurt ourselves, but that's not the case. Self-sabotage is more about our subconscious mind causing us to think in ways that keep us in a place it believes is safe, but it's not that we're safe. We're just staying in the same place, doing the same things over, and over, and over again.

# THE BACK STORY

Let me give you a little bit of background about what had been going on with me, what I had been thinking, and why I became involved in this project.

It had been a very interesting month or two. What I mean by "interesting" is that a lot had been happening in my life, all good stuff, great things had been happening. Our business was moving forward in a meaningful way. We'd created a wealth of new material. We were doing new seminars and coaching events that were well attended, successful by any measure.

The last thing that I really wanted to do was to create another project, if you will, to interject a project in the middle of the year, until I saw something. What I saw disappointed and disturbed me. I'm just going to tell you what it was.

I was watching people who had had moderate to good success start to slip backward. In some cases, they were going backward in big and unfortunate ways. I was really thinking about it and wondering what was going on with these individuals. Of course, I had no simple quick answer to it. I didn't know if I should get involved, do something, or teach something. I just let it rest.

I went away for Memorial Day weekend. Erin and I went away with some friends. We spent three or four days on a big lake just relaxing, boating and having a good time.

I realized in the moment, "I really do enjoy boating." I've always liked being on the water. I was raised boating, fishing and being on the water. It brought me back to a time around 1993 where I had an opportunity to attend my very first seminar.

Like many people when these things come into your life, I thought, "This is such a great opportunity. I have to go but I don't have the money to go."

In 1993, it was $3,500 to go to this seminar. It was a Tony Robbins event. It was in Ohio, but I lived in Chicago. I remember thinking to myself, "I have to go to this. I want to go to this so much." I felt so drawn.

I'm sure all of you have had that experience where you really feel drawn to an event, seminar, program, or something. You're thinking to yourself, "I just don't have the money or cash flow right now to do that, but it seems like it's in my life for a reason." I was having that kind of experience.

I had already made leaps and bounds in my life in many areas. I was in the process of not trying to do that, which is where many people are coming from. I was trying to figure out why I had done it or how I had done it. How was I having the success that I was having?

I didn't own my own business. I was still working for someone, but I was making good money. I had a home. Things were very good. I had bought a boat. I had bought it on credit, was making payments, and had just paid it off that week.

I remember standing in my kitchen with a cup of coffee in my hand. I was thinking to myself, "I would really like to go to this seminar. I feel like I would get answers there that I'm looking for, but I don't have the money in the timeframe that I'm going to need it in order to go."

I was looking out the window and I saw my boat sitting in the driveway. I thought to myself, "You could sell your boat, and you'd have the money." Another voice in my head said, "You've worked all your life to be able to have something like this. Why would you sell it? That seems kind of silly."

I knew that a lot of my friends and people who were around me knew that I had always wanted a boat. I had finally gotten it and worked hard for it. It was paid off and it was mine. I thought, "No. If I could ever figure out what it is that I'm doing so that I can be conscious about it and control it, I could have as many boats as I want or whatever kind of boat that I want."

I decided on the spot that I was going to sell it, and I did. I sold it that week. I was able to pay for the seminar. I was actually able to buy a computer for myself and really begin the systematic process that was necessary to become a business owner. A lot of it was just self-teaching. I had done that.

Eighteen years later, here I was sitting out on Smith Mountain Lake in Virginia with friends and family. We were just having a great time. I really had not engaged the idea about buying a new boat since all those years ago when I sold the last one. I've thought about it from time to time. I thought, "I said I was going to do this." I never really did it.

I bought a car a few years back, an Aston Martin. As you might imagine, it's a wonderful car. It was an almost $200,000 car. I have a lot of fun with it; I enjoy it. The only reason I was able to buy it is that I have a successful business. I never really entertained the idea of a boat. I thought, "Why is this coming up now?" I really wasn't thinking about it.

To make a long story short, I realized that it had some significance and that it was coming into my life at the right moment.

We went and had lunch at one of those dock-and-dine places where you pull up with your boat and tie up at one of a bunch of different slips. You get out and go to a restaurant. This boat pulled up next to me that I just absolutely fell in love with. A week later, after we got home, I bought one myself.

I thought, "I really like that. I could take the kids out tubing and waterskiing. We could put a bunch of people on it and go to dinners." I just really enjoyed being on the water. I had forgotten how much I really liked that.

I started thinking, "Money is really such a blessing in a person's life when they understand it and when it's used for the right things. It can be such a terrible burden, almost like a curse, for people who don't."

# FINANCIAL FREEDOM

I've heard repeatedly from all the different people I've coached in my career, that one of the best pieces of advice that I've given, the thing that they've heard me say that was really transformative for them was simply this: Financial freedom is not about how much money you can save in the bank. Financial freedom is being able to create whatever amount of money you need whenever you need it.

Let's say that you're doing very well, whatever that means to you. All of a sudden, you lose everything. If you have what I define as financial freedom, you're instantly able to go out and do it again. You can meet your needs. If you need money to pay the bills, pay the doctor, buy a new car, put tires on your car, buy a home, send your kids to school, go on a vacation, take that honeymoon or whatever it might be, you have the ability to do that right now.

Everybody has the ability to do it. Very few people ever get to the level of consciousness where they're aware by intention of how to do it. The great thing is that once you become consciously aware of how to do it, you never go back.

I'd been saying that for years. Here I am watching people go backward. I thought to myself, "Now, this is really interesting. Why would these people be going backward? What is actually going on with them?"

I recognized that one of the things that had happened in the industry that I'm a part of and in business in general is that people start to make a lot of money. Unfortunately, their money-making maturity is not mirrored in spiritual, psychological, or emotional growth.

I'm sure you will agree that people can be really screwed up and still make a lot of money. We see evidence of that all over the world in just about every different career you can imagine.

People can be a damn mess, but still have the ability to earn a lot of money because the principles required to earn money are different from the principles required to achieve many other things.

You really can be a jerk and make a lot of money. You can be the nicest guy on the block and make a lot of money. You can be very spiritual and make a lot of money. You can deny the existence of spiritual principles and make a lot of money. The requirement is that you're following the principles that make a lot of money.

The people I'm watching who have gone backward are getting themselves into a lot of trouble. What is actually happening with them is that ego took over somewhere. They didn't mature.

I received advice that probably has saved me many times that goes along with maturing. Years ago, my mentor said to me, "David, when you start to get the success that you're after and you really start to help a lot of people, people are going to say and write great things about you. It will be in the news and on TV. It will be here and there. People will talk about it.

"The uninformed or the person who is not totally mature will come from a place of kind of defying what you've done. In other words, they make you more special than you actually are." I think we see this with stars and celebrities. We view them as gods in a way. We really give them more power than they actually have.

This comes from wounded people and the idea that any one person is more special, gifted, or talented than someone else. The fact is that that's not true. We all have an equal amount of talent, gifts, and potential. The only difference is what one person does with it as opposed to what another person does with it.

Watching this take place is a little bit disturbing. It's not that these people forgot how to earn money. What happened is they became caught up in how great everybody else was saying they are.

In some cases, the examples become frighteningly extreme. You'll see people start cults and attract disciples. It gets crazy. It occurs when a person doesn't stay grounded. They don't know how to stay grounded. The wounded side of them really buys into to how great everybody is telling them that they are, and they feed off it as if it were a drug. Sometimes they begin to need it like a drug.

The advice that I got was, "The day you start to believe your own press clippings," in other words, the day you start to believe what everybody else says about you, "is the day that you start going down. That is the day you actually start going backward." You're not making decisions from the right place anymore in your life or your business.

You're making decisions to try to feed that insatiable ego hunger. The ego just wants more attention, recognition, and appreciation. It's a nasty thing. The problem is that it progresses from there to a place where the person believes that they have power that they don't have.

Many people over the years may have heard me talk about the idea that when you're wounded and have these areas of insecurities in your life, that insecurity speaks to you. It attempts to get things for your life, things that are not healthy. It tells you things that are not healthy.

The insecurity leads you outside yourself to places where you're trying to get some kind of fulfillment.

11

Unfortunately, an outside source can't possibly fulfill you. It may fulfill you in the moment, kind of like drugs and alcohol that make you feel better in the moment or maybe make you forget how you feel. The next day you're always feeling like crap because you overindulged in something. In the same way, people are starting to experience the consequences of this.

I was thinking that the problem that is here, and we have to be very careful with this, is that people need to mature in this area. They have not matured. They need to.

I hope they're not in a place where they can't hear somebody try to help them. Some of them are. Some of them actually are in a place where they can't hear it. They'll actually turn around and say, "You're trying to keep me down and hold me back. You don't believe in my vision and where I want to go." They're in for big setbacks.

When they experience these setbacks, one of the other damaging things that you'll hear them say is that they're spirit-led; God wants them to go in this direction. Nothing could be further from the truth. Because they're so drunk on their ego binge, they actually believe it themselves. It's very unfortunate and maybe a little sad.

I was thinking about all of this. It was leading me toward thinking about money on a global basis. The original reason why I got into the market that

I'm in is that I truly believe that the number-one way that we communicate on a global basis is by business.

With all the prejudices we have, many of us, many countries and communities, would not communicate with each other if it weren't for business. Business has broken down many barriers. Commerce has encouraged communication and cooperation.

What we're suffering from still is that the majority of the world remains in poverty. That is not a good thing. The only reason the majority of the world is still in poverty is in large part what we've been told about money and business. Frankly, the stories that we carry around within ourselves are what actually keep us in that place.

I was working with several other industries some years ago when I decided that I was going to make a conscious shift in the individuals I wanted to work with. I believed that people who are really stepping up to being an entrepreneur or a business owner have the greatest ability right now. That ability was primarily the result of current global communication capabilities. That would have most significant difference in the way our planet is moving.

In order to do that, you've have to be able to make a significant difference in your own life first. It's not just a difference. You have to go down that path of maturing in what it is that you're doing.

You have to be responsible in those areas of your life so that the message that you're giving to other people when you communicate and do business with them is one that you have it together. It's not fake or hype. You must actually have it together. People will admire that quality so much that they want to make a change in their own lives.

I truly believe to my core that money is an unbelievable miracle that has come into the human experience in a time where we could not grow as spiritual human beings without it.

# BRINGING MONEY INTO YOUR LIFE

The first two things I want to talk to you about are how you bring money into your life, step by step, when you absolutely need it, and then what some of the things are that are holding you back.

If you're serious about building a business or making a change in your life, there are a couple of things to understand. First, you have to understand money. Second, you must understand how to continually bring the money into your life that you need so it's not just the fast, cash injection type of idea but consistent cash flow. You want that money there month after month.

How do you handle your own growth responsibly? I'm going to take you on a very interesting journey. It will be something you've probably never heard before, and likely that you've never experienced before.

In order to bring money into your life quickly and really understand the fast-cash formula, you have to expand your mind to allow yourself to let that in so that you can do it.

It's not about saying, "Give me the step-by-step. What do I do? Do I make more phone calls, learn how to market, or get a different strategy?" Those things could take place. Very often, those things are necessary. Nothing works until your mind is expanded with the new idea of being able to bring money into your life at whatever amount you need and as fast as you need it.

I want you to think about this. If you had a little magic box in your home that produced whatever you wanted, what would happen to your state of consciousness, thoughts, and feelings whenever you opened the lid?

The first thing that would happen would be a complete change in your thinking. Think about this. All fear, worry, lack, and sense of insecurity would go out of it. Knowing that you could go to your little box as often as you need it would definitely eliminate all sense of limitation and strain from your mind.

When we're given problems and need money, we start to worry, struggle, tighten the purse strings, and do things that actually push the money away from us. Not only does it push the money away from us, but also it pushes away the ideas that would bring the money in. It changes our perceptions so that we actually can't see where the money is.

We have to know that, based on the Law of Polarity, if you have a need or a desire, the opposite of that has to exist in your life. That means that whatever you need or desire is already here in your life, and it's in your life in a way where all you have to do is reach out and grab it.

I literally tell people, "The money that you want, the thing that you desire, is as close as your own breath. It's not far away. It doesn't require great amounts of learning or strategy."

I'm not talking about futuristically. Let's say you're in a place where you're earning $100,000 a year or less now, and you want to earn $10 million. The $10 million is different.

You will definitely need a different way of "doing & being" from what you are right now, but you cannot have the problem that you have right now without the way for it to be fixed to also be present in your life because they go hand in hand.

If you knew you could go to the little black box as often as you needed, it really would eliminate all sense of limitation because the box would give you whatever you wanted whenever you wanted it. There would be no more poverty in your life.

Having what you wanted when you wanted it would not only lift you above the plane of material need, but if the power were used wisely, it would make you a better, more useful and more effective person.

How is it that we do that? The first thing is to understand that you have a need or desire. What I would like you to do right now is write down on a sheet of paper what it is that you need or desire. What we need to know at this point is the difference between a need and a want.

This is the critical first step in bringing the money in fast. You must know the difference between need and want. Then you must know how that difference actually affects you bringing in money. Let me take a minute to talk about this.

We're talking about money here. A need is based on what is reality in your life right now. How much do you need? I'm often astounded by this. Many people I ask this question don't know. They'll say, "I need $10,000, $5,000, or $100,000."

I'll say, "Is that to the penny?"

They say, "No."

When you answer in that way that you don't know, the number you're picking is not coming from a place of what you need. What you need is what you need, period. That means that you have to go in and look at how much money you need to the penny.

When you do that, you're dealing with a real number. That number was created out of whatever it was that you did in your life to create that need.

Whatever the number is, it is exactly what you need to the penny. I want you to think. it need it for a reason. You've created some kind of situation or circumstance in your life that for which you actually need that money. It's something that you've done, something for which you must accept responsibility.

You may be thinking, "Yes, but I need the money because something happened in my life that I have to respond to financially." It's the same thing. It's in your life. You are intimately and energetically connected with it. It's absolutely 100% real. This understanding is crucial.

When you have a want, the want is something that is real but generally comes from another place energetically. Let's say a person's need is $4,832.25. That would pay off their immediate bills, get them back on track to paying their bills on time next month, or whatever it may be.

They want $10,000. The thing about this that's significant is that most people want the $10,000 out of fear and because they don't want to have to deal with the debt anymore. They want some breathing room and don't want to have to experience whatever it is that they're experiencing that they don't like.

All of that is coming from an energetic place of lack in a person's life. It's not something that you need.

It's something that you want, and that is from a place of fear.

Frequently, I'll ask people, "How much money do you want to make?" They'll say, "$1 million," "$10 million" or "I just want to be financially free."

When they say those things, it's coming from the place of never wanting to have to deal with money again because there has been so much stress in their lives. They've witnessed so much pain and heartache, and have struggled for so long. They wish that they could win the damn lottery and not have to deal with money anymore.

Energetically, it's coming from the wrong place. What happens is that instead of bringing the opportunity into their lives to get that much money, they're creating opportunities that would actually take it away because it's coming from fear.

They get what they're energetically equal to. It doesn't matter what the picture of the number is because that picture is created in our conscious minds. What's important to know is that it's coming from the subconscious where the powerhouse of energy is being stored to bring something in or push something away. We'll get what we fear in that case.

This is why it's important to know what you need. This is the difference between needing and wanting. You can have everything that you want in your life if you will understand and learn how to manifest what you need first. It's also the fastest way to get what you want.

Most people are thinking to themselves, "I don't want to take the long road." You're already taking the long road because you don't know how to understand how to do this right now, where you are. You're making it take a long time by trying to go in different directions. You have to come from the place of what you need first.

Once you learn how to bring in what you need whenever you need it, you actually start to build a couple of things that make the thing that you want much easier to bring in. First, you start to build belief.

If manifesting money, bringing in the quick cash, is not something that you're accustomed to doing, or at the level that you actually need it, then the one problem you're actually fighting is a belief system that you don't have but are trying to get.

You intellectually understand that it's possible, but you don't actually have the belief system to back up what you need. Energetically, you're creating more of the same. This creates struggle in a person's life.

You must change your belief system. Once you do this, the next things that begin to change are your faith and confidence. Numerous people will say, "I have great faith," but they really don't have faith. What they have is stored knowledge based on things that they know they can do when they don't necessarily know the outcome, but it really isn't faith.

Real, strong faith is based on understanding principles that have to do with faith. When you understand those principles, you become an unbelievable powerhouse in what you're able to do because you no longer have to walk around and trust everything that you see. You actually know the true cause of what brings into your life whatever it is that you need.

Money is an effect. It is not a cause, but people walk around and treat it like a cause. That's part of the problem. It's an effect. That means that if you are employing the causes in your life, the effect must happen.

If you take a rock, hold it in your hand, and drop it, it's always going to go down. Why? It's because gravity is always pulling anything heavier than air towards the center of the Earth. It's an absolute law.

That means that if you follow the law, it's going to work exactly as it is supposed to work. If you're going to try to do something outside of the law, you're going to experience the effects of it whether you like it or not.

If we're viewing money as a cause or something that happens outside of our own control, then we're subject to the effects of worry, struggle, and having bad financial times in our lives because we don't understand the cause of what allows us to bring the money in every single time when we need it.

Think about it like this. How would your life really change if you didn't have to worry about money anymore? It's not just your physical life. Obviously, you'd be able to go out and buy things, but that's not the most important thing. What kind of freedom would you have if you didn't have to worry about money anymore?

Could you imagine what it would be like to lift that mental pressure off of yourself and not have that emotional weight if you didn't have to worry about it and knew that, if you just did specific things day in and day out, that money would come in with great abundance every time? If something went wrong, you would instantly know how to change it.

That would be the most unbelievable gift you could ever give yourself. You are in control of giving yourself that. The first thing is to understand the difference between a need and a want.

You have already written down the amount that you need. If you don't know, that's fine. When you take a break from reading this book, calculate exactly how much it is that you need. Then write that number down.

# WHY YOU NEED THE MONEY

The second step is to understand why you need that money. Why do you need it? You may say, "Why is that the second step?" The reason it is the second step is, whatever reason you've created until this point has not been a good enough reason for anything to change.

Chances are that if you need money right now, you've probably needed it for some time. This is not a new story in your life. It's a recurring story. It may be a recurring story in your family. Here, in this moment, you have the opportunity to change that story forever. You have to get down to the real why of why it is that you need it.

If you say, "I need it because I need to pay my bills," that's not good enough. People go about their lives all of the time without paying their bills. I've seen people create some of the most unbelievable catastrophes in their lives because their "why" for doing something wasn't strong enough.

I'll tell you what my "why" was. My "why" for making a change in my life really was that I did not want to leave a legacy to my family or anybody else in this world based on the direction that I was going. I absolutely needed to know that the principles I had been hearing about were real.

25

Like everybody else who has read to this point, if you're receiving this information, you're receiving this information for a reason. No, the fact that you are reading this book is not a coincidence. You're reading it because a part of you wants to do something with it.

You have the ability to make significant changes in your life, your family's life, and in everybody's life that you touch, but you're receiving the gift right now, and not someone else. The question is if you're going to do something with it.

That was the question for me. I thought, "Do you know something, David? I don't want to go to my grave not knowing and not getting to that place." I did not want to pass that on to my kids or other people. Prior to that, I had bills, debt, and all kinds of problems, and the pain of experiencing those problems still was not enough to change them.

What will it be for you? Why do you want to make this change? Why do you want to bring this cash in and fulfill this need right now? What would get you energetically excited enough to make a mini breakthrough? You don't need a huge breakthrough. You just need a mini breakthrough that will take you to a big breakthrough.

Further along in the book, we're going to talk about what's actually holding you back and how to identify that. Right now, though, why do you want to have the breakthrough? It's very important to know.

You need to know. If you're having any problems with money or your business, knowing that is going to be a step toward changing those problems. You will learn how to make more money in your business. Perhaps more importantly, you will learn how to rewrite your money stories. If you don't rewrite your money stories, you have to understand how much of your business and your life it actually affects.

One of the things people are having a terrible time with is hiring good people, keeping those people, and getting people who are productive, and it's causing terrible problems in their business. This all has to do with a person's money story.

You will learn how to actually make the changes you need to make and where it's being created in your money story where money is constantly fluctuating in such a way as to cause you to panic every month. Panic is not necessary.

Your maturity level around money is going to make a significant difference. It must make a significant difference because if you are coming from a place of this spiritual milquetoast idea that is running rampant out there, you're really in a lot of trouble.

I have watched people take my message, my teachings over the last few years and completely water it down so that everybody they're around will be able to accept it, with their wounds, without having to change anything. It's frankly not a good thing because people are getting a mixed message and learning things that are not accurate.

Somebody told me, "One of the interesting things about the coaching industry is that people are getting to the point where they don't respect the coaches anymore." I think that's very true. One of the reasons is many things that are being taught are just completely inaccurate. You cannot take fixed principles and then adjust them to fit where you don't want to grow. It won't work.

This is about learning something that most people really have no idea is there or how it works. When you're talking about the miracle of money, you have to understand that money really is a miracle. If you don't view it as a miracle or understand how the principles of that miracle actually work, you're really subject to not having the abundance flowing into your life on a regular basis. When it's not flowing in your life, you sure feel it. This will not only change your cash, but it will change your business.

If you don't have a business yet, even more reason to understand and change, because people who don't have a business are really subject to what somebody else is paying them. I want to show you how to break free of that so that you're not stuck in that slavery for the rest of your life. Then you can get to the point where you really can start your own business, or take whatever idea you have and learn how to monetize it. If you don't understand the laws, you're really going to be in a lot of trouble.

We talked about the need versus the want. We talked about how much you actually need in your life. The next nugget of knowledge is something that often causes people to give me funny looks when I talk about it, but you really have to understand the significance of it.

When you have a belief, your subconscious mind is designed to get you to see things with your eyes and perception in a way that is in harmony with the protection of that belief. That means that if something exists outside yourself, it will allow you to make a significant change. Your subconscious mind's job is to keep you from seeing it.

That sounds crazy, and I'll admit that the first time I heard it I thought, "That's really whacky." Then I had a very significant example of that in my own life that allowed me to go from $20,000 a year to $60,000 a year in a very short time. However, prior to that I couldn't see the opportunity because my subconscious mind wouldn't let me. That's what its job is.

When a person tells me, "I need to make a specific amount of money," you have to realize that the money is already there, but you just can't see it.

This gets crazy. I actually had somebody tell me that the only reason that I had success was because in numerology the numbers in my name added up to a certain number. The ideas that people are buying into are keeping them right where they are. That numerology idea is so ludicrous it isn't even funny.

God did not make one person more special than another one. Nobody has any gift or name that is going to make him or her more successful than another person is.

You have to know that you're programmed to see whatever your mind says to see to try to keep you in that place that you are. You also need to know that the law says the money you need is also present in your life now. The question is where is it?

If you're going to begin to discover where that cash is in your life, you have to make a decision that you're going to believe in these principles at least long enough to make a change. If you're going to flip-flop in your head, it's never going to work.

One day you're thinking, "I'm going to do this. I'm going to get the money and follow what David is teaching." The next day you're thinking, "I don't feel like it. Maybe there's something else causing the problem. I don't know if I believe this."

You go back and forth, and the result is your subconscious accomplished exactly what it was designed to accomplish. It kept you right where you were, and it kept you from moving forward. In your life, all that you're experiencing is the craziness and confusion around it. You don't want to stay where you are, but your subconscious mind's job is to hold you where you are. That means you have to be able to see something that you currently can't see.

Napoleon Hill talked about this in Think and Grow Rich. He called it the "sly disguises of opportunity." When you need something, the opportunity always shows up, but it often comes disguised as something you don't want. It's because your subconscious mind has to tell you to stay away from it, so it gets very confusing. You have to ask, "Does the opportunity have the ability to get me what I want?" Forget what else it represents.

So again: If you're going to begin to discover where that cash is in your life, you have to make a decision that you're going to believe in these principles at least long enough to make a change. So, answer the questions: Why do you need this money? Why do you need to make a change?

# WHAT'S HOLDING YOU BACK

We're going to isolate the thing that's holding you back from having already made the changes necessary to bring in the amount of money you need. The thing that's holding you back is the "money story" (the circumstance) that your subconscious mind projects out into your reality, into the universe, to trick you into believing it's real. Any opportunity that shows up, you will see as the money story that's holding you back and not as the potential that it has.

Going back to my personal path that I shared with you, I saw the Tony Robbins seminar I told you about as something that I really wanted to do, but I couldn't do it because I would have had to sell my boat. That was the first thought I had in my mind. I didn't have the money. I was going to have to sell something that I loved. That seems crazy in the moment, but it's exactly how it works. It always shows up as something you don't want or you don't want to experience.

It's an illusion because the thing you want is right on the other side of that experience Ö it's right on the other side of releasing the ONE thing that is holding you back. That's the darndest thing about it. I don't care what you need, how badly you need it, or what kind of struggle you're going through. If you need it, the solution is absolutely there, and it's there right now. I guarantee it, no matter what anybody else has told you. I'd stake my life on it. My whole purpose in life is to help people see that basic concept.

To wrap this up, the solution is appearing to you as something that you can't do or don't want. And your subconscious is holding you back by projecting a money story (a reason) that the opportunity is a bad idea or an impossibility. I want you to realize that the thing that you want is on the other side of rejecting that lie.

What opportunities are showing up in your life that would allow you to get the amount of money written on the sheet of paper that you actually need? Next to that, I want you to write what it is about the opportunities that you don't want to experience. Is the opportunity going to cost you money? Is it going to be risky in some way? Is it going to threaten to be humiliating or embarrassing? Does it cause you to be uncomfortable?

Once you identify those things, it will allow you to walk through the illusion and get the money on the other side. If you do that and take action on that opportunity, instantly it'll be there. It's there every time. It doesn't fail. Gravity always pulls to the center of the Earth. The ball always drops to the center of the Earth. It's absolute; it never fails.

We have to identify some of these things to know how to see past the illusion and actually break through it. It's not about breaking through once. It's about doing it continuously day after day. Your life can be amazing where money is no longer an issue, and you can actually do in your business and your life what you were put here to do, which is to create and be of service to other people.

Remember that money is a tool to be used. That's all it's here for. It's to make your life and other people's lives better. It's to expand God's purpose and the universe, and it couldn't be done without money.

Before we move onto the second part where we'll discover the roadblocks you've put in your path, let's do a brief recap. You really must wrap your mind around the idea that whatever problem you have in your life, the solution already exists, and it exists in your life right now (not in the future). It's not something that is outside of your life that's on the other side of the world or that requires you to search for it. It already exists, and it's already close to you in your life.

The best way I can describe it to you is that it is as close to you as your breath. That means it doesn't matter what the problem is. The laws never change. We often have heard people say, "Have you learned anything new? What are you studying now versus what you studied 20 years ago?" I learn new things every day, and I study every day.

What people really don't grasp is that the laws that govern the entire universe don't change. They are fixed. Those are the laws of life.

What changes and what is constantly changing is our understanding of those laws. The more that we understand them and become aware of the power and possibilities that lie within them and how we relate to them, the more we can use them in our life.

Think back about 30 or 40 years ago to about 1960 or 1970. You'll realize that if you look back at that timeframe in history, things were moving. History was moving, and advancements in technology were moving at a good clip. There was a great deal of activity. There was movement in the world, the economic world, in societies and religion. There were all kinds of changes happening, but it's nothing compared with the speed of today's movement.

If you look at how long it took to get something done then versus today, it's like a million years. That's how fast we're moving ahead. Why are we moving ahead that fast? It's because we understand the laws more.

With all of the technology we currently have, the way to do all of that has always been here. It was here when we were back in the caves and making tools from sticks and rocks. The laws that create the computer were always here. They were there then. The difference is that we were not aware of them.

# THE LAW OF POLARITY

One of the greatest things of the last few generations is that we're becoming more and more aware that there is a law that exists that governs the overcoming of all problems. That is the Law of Polarity.

The Law of Polarity states that everything has an opposite, and it's equal and opposite. That means that no matter what problem you have, the exact opposite of that problem also must exist within the problem itself. The great possibility that lies there is that we can change the results that we have in our life instantaneously.

I don't say that to be hypey or markety because it's not either of those things. It's actually real. What takes a long time is a person being able to wrap his or her mind around the concept, but it doesn't have to take a long time. That goes into what's holding you back.

The difficulty is wrapping your mind around a new idea. The idea is that no matter what problem you're having, the solution is simultaneously present in your life.

The darnedest thing about this is that because your mind is programmed, the programming, which is your belief system, controls your perception. That perception controls the way we view our outside world. We will view our outside world in accordance with that belief system.

That means we only see or perceive what we believe to be true. That then becomes real to us. That becomes our reality. That sets our limits. The problem is that this is how we're trained to go through our life, by dealing with what is reality.

That's how we learned all through school. That's how we learned from all the people in authority in our life. It was to deal with things in a realistic and responsible fashion as to how we respond and react to those things.

When you hear talk about a higher law, realize that most people don't really understand it. It's obvious they don't understand it from observing the situation that the world is in currently. People will often look at you as if you just fell out of a tree if you try to tell them to believe something other than dealing with what's in their life and trying to convince them that they can actually change it.

Is this concept new? No, it's not new. Through all of history, whether you're reading the Bible, the Koran, the Bhagavad Gita, the Torah or any of the major philosophers that were in the world and all of the self-help industry, they have been based on one primary concept. That is, "If you believe it, you can have it."

I built an entire career about teaching people how to change their beliefs in order to change their lives because the moment you change the belief, everything in your reality begins to shift. That means that whatever you're experiencing, you will stop experiencing that and start experiencing the polar opposite of it.

Here's the key to this. All of our life up to this very moment, our belief system was really created by the experiences that we had in different circumstances with different results and different conditions that were happening around us. Then we determined some way or another that those things were true and real. We got emotionally involved in those experiences. Boom. We have a belief system.

In order to change a belief system, something different has to happen. As adults, when we begin to change a belief system, we have to realize that the way we change it is based largely on our evaluation of something.

I'm not just talking about something that we just intellectually understand, but it's a deep belief. That means not only do we think that it's true, but we emotionally respond as if it's true and our actions are in accordance with both of those things, our thoughts and our emotions. We act on those things every day. We also get the results of those things.

This is how it works: If you're having a problem bringing money into your life, you believe that at some level you shouldn't have money in your life. You will think to yourself, "I sure wish that was different." That's completely different. That's not a belief. That's a wish or a want. That only takes place in your conscious thinking, but it's not integrated into who you are.

Don't feel bad about it. It's not integrated in most people. I think it's some crazy number, like 1% of the people on the planet earn 96% of all the income. You have to ask yourself why that is.

We're trying to wrap our minds around a new concept that is going to make a change. That is to expand your mind because you have to expand into something. You can't experience something new on the outside if you haven't experienced it on the inside. That's where you must get it first. You must get it on the inside first.

Now we know the first step is to determine how much you need. It's not what you want but how much you need. We know the second is to determine why you need it. Those were both most important to know before we move to the third step.

The third step is to recognize or become aware of the opportunity that exists around you right now to bring that money into your life. This is usually the first big stumbling block: becoming aware of what that opportunity actually is.

We have to ask ourselves why that is. The answer is that we're not programmed to see the opportunity. We're programmed to see something else.

It's like Napoleon Hill aptly described in Think and Grow Rich. He explained that people who have problems with money don't see the opportunities that exist to bring in money. They see those exact opportunities as more problems. They see them as things they can't do. They see them as all kinds of struggle and difficulty in life. They don't actually see these things as opportunity.

Knowing the Law of Polarity will allow you to see the other side of something. You may look at an opportunity that's coming into your life right now and say, "I really can't do this because," and then you supply a reason why you can't. If I use the Law of Polarity, I am empowered to look at the other side of the same circumstances and say, "If I did do it, it could make a change in my life here. I literally could bring in the money."

Which brings us to the fourth step:

The fourth step is, once you've determined what the opportunity is, you must take action on that opportunity. That means you are going to totally step into the opportunity. It doesn't matter what happens next.

At this point, you may confront one of life's greatest pitfalls. We start to project out in our mind, "If I take advantage of this opportunity, what's going to happen next?"

It's as if we want to control the opportunity, but we don't actually see the ridiculousness of that. If you're going to step into a new opportunity that's going to bring you the things that you want, you have to know that it's going to cause you to grow and do different things.

There are things that you're going to have to change. You couldn't possibly know what those changes are or what those experiences would be like because you've never had the opportunity before. To try to project in your mind what that is or how it's going to work just keeps holding you back further because it creates doubt and fear in your life.

Those doubts turn into fear, which quickly turns into anxiety. Before we know it, we're actually doing nothing. We're just sitting around thinking about what we should be doing.

From time to time, someone asks, "Is this finally going to be the program that makes a change for me?" To me, that's really a very interesting question. It really coincides with some of the things we went over a few pages ago. It's worth mentioning again. So many people out there have taken good principles and have not taught them in a way that will empower somebody to make a change in their life.

The reason that they haven't done that is because they've taken the principle, they like the concept of the principle and they want to teach the principle themselves, but they don't actually make the change themselves.

What they do is actually attract people on the same level as them, and it almost becomes kind of like a community gathering versus anybody actually making any changes. If I'm afraid to change, how can I help you make a change? I can't, so we're both going to stay stuck.

That's one reason people ask the question about whether "this time" this opportunity or this program will "work". You may not think you have experienced it, but you have. You've probably gone where you think it's going to be comfortable for you to go instead of where you're actually going to get growth, and, of course, you haven't experienced the growth.

There's another thing that happens, and this has happened forever. This is not something that's new. Because our subconscious mind wants to keep us where we are, we're always looking for the easy way to change something.

We want the magic pill, the magic button, the magic formula, and the magic system. We want something that is going to allow us to get what we want but is not going to cause us to be very uncomfortable and is not going to make us change at all.

We only see what we want to see when it comes to sales and marketing copy. Then we buy something, like a program that teaches us how to do something with our business or make some change in our life. The second that it gets to us having to make a change, we stop right there and say, "The program didn't work for me."

The program doesn't really do anything at all. In fact, if you just put it on your shelf, it will sit there for all eternity and it will never do anything. It will just sit there. The thing is that if you don't make a change on the inside, that program that you purchased is never going to be able to work its magic.

I think many programs out there are phenomenal. They have incredible ways to take their businesses to places that you probably only see in your imagination right now, but they're never going to work for you if you haven't grown into them. It's just plain and simple. They won't.

It's like giving a 5-year-old the keys to a Ferrari. There's nothing wrong with the Ferrari. A Ferrari has incredible performance, and it does every time it's driven by the right person. If you give it to a person who doesn't know how to operate it, a person who is inexperienced, you've turned a beautiful piece of art that handles unbelievably into a death trap.

When people go out there and buy all of these programs they haven't grown into, that's exactly what they've done. It's almost like a death trap because they just sit on their shelf collecting dust. They never use them. They start to get negative about how they feel about them because they actually haven't made a change inside themselves.

Then they start saying, "It didn't work for me, and it wasn't the right thing for me. I'm looking for something different." They perpetually get on this train of looking for something different and not understanding that the change has to come from within.

How do we make that change within? In other words, what is it that's holding you back?

Here's what's important. We really must understand a couple of things. First, our subconscious mind works perfectly 24 hours a day. The way that it's designed to work is that once it gets a belief locked into it, its job is to hold the belief and carry that belief out in your life, no matter what happens. That's what its job is.

Examine carefully your life and the lives of people that you know, things that you see on the internet, and things that you see happening all over the world. I think that you and I would both agree that we see people do some stupid stuff. Some of the things make you sit there and say, "I cannot believe that people are actually doing this." It's really stupid stuff.

They have the exact same ability to think as you or I do, but they're getting a completely different result. Why is that? Is it because they don't know how to think? No. Actually, they're thinking perfectly, but they're thinking perfectly along the lines of how they've been programmed, and they cannot think any differently.

Have you ever said to yourself, "Why is it that that person did that to me?" and then you get upset with the person that did whatever it was to you? We think to ourselves, "They had a choice. They know the difference between right and wrong, yet they still did wrong."

That indicates that they really don't know the difference. They wouldn't be doing it if they actually knew and had embodied that into who they were. That's not what they've embodied. They've embodied something else. We actually fault people for being programmed the wrong way, and they're almost powerless to change it unless they have different way to make an evaluation. That's the key.

If we have new information that we can evaluate, then we can create a new belief system that will empower us. Napoleon Hill pointed out that it doesn't take any more effort to aim high in life or bring things into your life that you really want than it does to accept misery or poverty.

The energy that creates one is the same energy that creates another. The same energy that has you where you are right now is precisely the same energy that you will use to create a life of your dreams, whatever it is that you want.

You have to stop and ask yourself a question. It's a serious question. Here's what the question is: Have you ever spent serious time thinking about why you get the results that you get?

Most people walk around and think to themselves, "I want different results. I want better results," or they complain and moan about the result that they getting, but they don't spend much time saying, "I wonder why I'm getting the results that I'm getting."

That would actually lead them to a more constructive answer, but that's not how the subconscious mind works. The subconscious mind has to do something to deflect you away from the current answer and to keep you going down these rabbit holes so that you can't change it.

Its programing believes that if you change it, it's going to die and that's the last thing that it wants to do. As long as the programing is keeping you alive, in the moment it thinks, "Right on. We're doing the exact right thing perfectly," but because you are a thinking person, it has to do things to warp the way that you evaluate different things that come into your life so that you could perceive them as something you don't want so you don't have to change.

Here's a case in point in my own life. I was living next door to a drug dealer, I was married, and I had two children. We were on food stamps and living in the equivalent of the projects, or pretty darn close to it.

For two years, I was living this way. I was so ashamed at how I was living and that I had let myself get into that place and completely stuck as to how to change it that I could not see the opportunity that existed around me for those two years that would have literally catapulted me out of that existence.

It wasn't until I started asking myself the question, "Why am I getting the results that I don't want?" that I actually got the right answer that made the change that allowed me to see the opportunity that had been around me for two years to take my income from $20,000 to $62,000 and take me out of that situation.

I want you to think about this. How many of you have been going through your life, dealing with the results that you're currently getting in your life, wishing that it could change and wondering what it is that is holding you back?

A difference exists between saying, "Why am I getting the results that I'm getting?" and "What is it's holding me back?" Frequently, I hear this question from people, "What is it that's holding me back?"

I'm about to tell you what it is that's holding you back, but it's not going to be what you think it is. That's how crazy our subconscious mind is.

Remember, as simple as it may sound, your subconscious mind is extremely effective. It has to keep you focused on the wrong thing in order to keep you where you are so that you don't move forward and so that when the opportunity comes, you don't see it as an opportunity.

Actually, if you see any opportunity in it at all, you'll see all the reasons why you can't embrace it. "I don't have the money. I don't have the time. My spouse won't let me," or whatever. You'll talk yourself out of it as fast as you talked yourself into it. That's how you know your subconscious mind is working.

First off, have you said to yourself, "What is it that's holding me back?" Understand that it is taking you down the rabbit hole and that rabbit hole never ends. Then you start looking at what happened in your childhood. You try to remember what happened in your childhood. You start wondering if this person did this, or if that person did that, or what scarring experience you had. It is never ending.

Very often people can't remember, so they spend all of this time trying to remember. "I wish I could remember what happened. I know that I've got this block and something happened around the age of 4, 14, 3," or whatever it is.

They keep looking and looking while the subconscious mind is in the background shaking its head and saying, "Yes. It's working. We have them down the rabbit hole, and we can keep them there for 20 years. We can be on the psychiatrist's couch for 20 years. They'll just keep talking about the problem but never make a change."

Now we'll get back to what I was saying. The subconscious mind is actually doing its job. It is working and saying, "Yes! We're keeping them right where they are! Right where it's safe!"

# THE EXCUSE

People say, "What is it that's holding me back?" It's one word. Write this word down: "Excuse." That's what it is. The thing that is holding you back from moving forward is the excuse that you make in the moment as to why you can't do it. That's the only thing that's holding you back.

I want you to think about something. You really have to think about this. Very often, right after we make the excuse, we then engage our magnificent imagination to create something that doesn't really exist. We'll say, "I can't do this because I don't have the money, I don't have the time, and all this stuff happened in my past."

All of that stuff is in your imagination. It's not actually real. Some of you are thinking, "I don't have the money." That's not true. The Law of Polarity says that's not true. You do have the money. If you keep saying you don't, your subconscious mind wins again and you don't get to see it.

Where does it stop you from even getting to that point? It stops you at the excuse. Once you make the excuse, you don't have to do anything else. That's it. It's done. It's over. It's a fact. The idea has sunk into the ground. It's buried. You're not moving anywhere. That's what must change, what must disappear, the excuse.

This is one of the most fascinating things about the subconscious mind. Every individual has the perfect excuse for everything. What is that? It's when they say that they can't do something and the reason that follows next is their excuse. It is always perfect for them. It is the perfect reason to stop them from moving forward.

What do I mean by perfect? Let's examine that. It seems that it comes at the right time. It's totally logical. It is totally emotional. It is totally realistic in their mind that it's absolutely perfect, and they can't see any way around it. That's what makes it perfect. If you don't bring in some other knowledge about it, you could never get around it. It's the perfect trap. You're stuck.

Your subconscious mind doesn't say to you, "Excuse me, Mary or Joe, I know that you're trying to move forward in your life and you really want to achieve incredible things. However, I'm going to try to stop you, and here's how I'm going to do it. Let's see if you can catch it."

The subconscious mind doesn't do that. It has to engage you in the process so that you don't know that it's happening and that you actually become the excuse. That's exactly where you stop, and you don't move forward.

We can get into all kinds of talk about self-worth, whether you believe you're worthy of money, how you were raised regarding money, and the traumatic things that happened in your past. I'm sure that some or all of those things are true for you. Certainly, they were true for me.

I want you to know this. I stop and think to myself every once in a while, "David, when you teach, are you teaching things that you learned when you first changed or are things that you learned much later on that people can't apply until later on?"

I always try to bring myself back to asking, "What were the first things that you changed?" because you have to realize something. No one was more broke than I was. I owed more than I made, so I didn't even have any hope. I would have had to work forever. I made less than I owed, and I couldn't possibly ever pay it off. It was a losing scenario.

I had a terrible attitude. I didn't finish high school. I had a poor work record. I had a viewpoint on the world that was extremely negative, yet I was still in this place. Absolutely nothing was changing. How is it that I could increase my income from $20,000 to $62,000 in 30 days? How is it that could possibly happen if I didn't have any money and I had a bad attitude?

The only way that could happen is if it was there already, only I wasn't seeing it. That's the problem.

No matter what it is that you need, it's already there but you're just not seeing it. How do you get to the point where you can see it? You have to change your belief system to see it. That's the only way that you can see it.

You can change it temporarily and see an opportunity. If you don't change it permanently, you'll go into the opportunity, and then once you're in the opportunity, all of a sudden it will be like the walls close around you and you get stuck in the mire of the thoughts in your head because nothing on the inside has actually made a shift.

We discussed earlier that your belief system is based on your evaluation of something. You must change your belief system, which is controlling everything. Those people who are out there telling you that your belief has nothing to do with your result are crazy. Don't listen to them because nothing productive is ever going to come of that, absolutely nothing.

Your belief system has everything to do with your result. Your belief system is the equivalent of your results. We have undisputable facts to prove all over the world that changing the results does not change the belief system.

If you thrust a person into a different result, it's not going to change their belief system. Eighty-five percent of lottery winners are broke in five years. You can thrust a person into wealth, and they'll go right back to where their belief system says that they should be.

It's like a thermostat. If you set a thermostat at 72 degrees and the temperature drops lower than 72, the heat is going to come on and bring the temperature right to 72. If it gets hotter than 72, the air conditioner is going to come on and bring it right back to 72.

That's exactly how your subconscious mind works. If it's set for you to be at whatever level you're supposed to be at, if something around you begins to change, then it's going to kick up its ugly head, change your perception and bring you right back to where it is that you want it to be.

We see this with people and income all of the time. They get it up a little bit and all of a sudden everything in their life goes to hell in a hand basket, and they come right back down to where they were.

It's because they started to change their activity a little bit, but they never went in and changed the belief system. You must have it on the inside if you're going to have it permanently on the outside, and we do that by shifting our evaluation of something.

Here's an interesting example. I have been telling people for years to stop cutting coupons out. Stop living like there is not abundance. It's not just about saying you believe that the universe is abundant and then you cut coupons and are bickering and bartering for everything that you're buying, but actually living that abundance.

It's actually saying, "I'm not going to do that anymore. I want to be paid full price. I deserve to be paid full price for what I do, and I'm going to pay somebody else the same thing. I'm not looking for a deal.

There's a crazy coupon show on TV. Somebody asked me, "Have you watched it?" I said, "I wouldn't put that in my head if you paid me. I'm not watching it. It's very destructive. It's crazy."

A study that came out that says how negative an impact this show is actually having on people. It's not giving them hope or inspiration. It's entertainment about people who are poverty conscious and it is going to come back to bite people. There have been articles written that say the behavior is destructive, leading to loss of self-esteem. Putting ideas like that in your mind will be enormously destructive to your progress and will have a negative effect on your ability to move forward.

We must get the idea out of our mind that there is lack. That's why I created the program the Miracle of Money. We have to change our evaluation of money. You must change what you believe about money because money is an enormous problem in most people's lives. It's not just you or your neighbor. It is a global epidemic of a problem.

# MONEY, THE ROOT OF SO MUCH GOOD

We've learned that money is a bad thing, yet hard work is a good thing. So, let me ask you another question: What is it that we're working hard for? We're working hard for a bad thing. That actually puts us in a bad place ourselves.

Most people are spending their lives doing something they hate with people that they don't even like just for a few bucks. We're trading our life for money. We were never meant to trade our life for money, especially for a few dollars an hour. We were not meant to live that way.

We are God's greatest gift. We've got all of spirit's higher faculties, yet most people walk around and have no idea what they are let alone how to use them.

The things that we can do and create are phenomenal. You can be so far ahead of where you are six months or a year from now if you would start to entertain a new idea.

I've watched lives like this change all over the world with people that I've worked with for a very long period. I get together with people like Suzanne Evans, Alexandria Brown, and Fabienne Fredrickson, just to name a few people. One of the first things that they will say to me when we're getting together is, "David, I know that I've said this to you a million times, but I'm going to say it again. Thank you so much for what you taught me because my life would be nothing like it is now without that information."

They say it repeatedly. I've known these people for years, and they keep saying it. I think, "I just saw you last week and you told me the same thing." They say, "I just can't believe how much better it keeps getting. It keeps getting better because of what you taught me."

You have to understand something. It's not mine. This is universal knowledge. Somebody taught it to me. I'm as grateful to that person as they are to me because my life wouldn't be what it is without it.

What I have realized is that in order for it to change for you, you're going to have to reevaluate the thing that you've been taught was bad or not good all of your life, and that's money.

Money is a miracle. We could not be where we are today and we cannot get where we're going without understanding that money is actually a miracle in our life. Money was created to expand God's kingdom. It was not to destroy it, make it worse, or make it a god in and of itself but to expand that kingdom.

We're all part of the spiritual kingdom. We are spiritual beings in a physical body. We're spiritual beings having a physical reality. We're having a physical experience, and money is part of that experience.

People often try to say that the physical is no good. We're triune. We live on three planes of understanding at the same time. We're physical, intellectual, and spiritual. To say that one is more important than the other is or to try to push one away as being bad and make the other ones good is dangerous.

Where did those ideas come from? Those were not the ideas of the great philosophers. Those were not the ideas of the people who instituted the religions that are studied today. Those were ideas of limitation that the dictators and rulers got their hands on and then taught to everyone else. Here's the reason why. That other information sets you free. It does not keep you in bondage, which is where those rulers and dictators wanted people to be.

For those of you who live in a free country, what is the one thing that keeps you from being free? It's a lack of money, which is the only thing that enslaves you and subjugates you to someone else. Lack of money is what keeps you in slavery.

How does that happen? How could that be possible? It has been so insidious over the years that it has come to the point where you can get an opportunity placed right in front of you, and you'll instantly make an excuse not to do it and stay right where you are.

Why do you think we're moving ahead so fast in so many other things but we're not moving ahead fast in the money?

We are moving faster when it comes to money than we ever have before because there are more millionaires on the planet than there ever has been in history, but it's still relatively slow in comparison to all the other knowledge and technology that's actually going on out there.

The great thing about it is that once you get the awareness, you don't go backward. Once you become aware of how to breathe, you don't stop breathing. Once you become aware of how to eat, you don't stop eating. Once you become aware of how to ride a bike, you could not ride a bike for 20 years, get back on the bike, and away you go.

It's not memory. Memory is completely different from awareness. Most people learned how to swim when they were a kid. Take someone out of the pool and throw him or her back in 20 years later, and off he or she goes. You swim. You don't forget.

I've asked myself some things. As a kid, I wondered, "It seems like money is such an important thing in our life. What's the truth that so many people struggle with?" The first thing you have to ask yourself is, "Is money important or not?" It is. That is a fact that we can't change.

If you want to live a life where money is not important, then I would suggest that you get rid of everything you have, including your clothes, and move into the woods somewhere. Money is not the only important thing, but it touches everything that is important, just like air.

You have to think about this. It is very important. We absolutely need it to survive yet so few people master it. Why is that? It's because they're afraid of it. How in hell did we become afraid of it? Are you afraid of air? Are you afraid of pizza? We're not afraid to eat, breathe, or drink water. Why would we be afraid of money?

It's because many people in power didn't want to share that power. They believed that by making us afraid of money, ignorant about money, they wouldn't have to share power. If they could integrate the negativity into all the things that we're afraid of in religion, and attach money to things like shame, self-worth, humiliation, and all the emotions that we naturally as human beings want to avoid experiencing, they could keep all the money for themselves and we wouldn't have any. In fact, we would be enslaved to them to have to work.

You may say, "That's kind of a stretch." Is it really? Look around you. I'm not just making this up. This comes after years of doing research and studying history. If you go back into history, you can't come to any other conclusion. That's exactly what happened.

What are you going to do to change it? What are you going to do to make the shift? The first thing is ask, "What's holding me back?" I told you what's holding you back. It's the excuse.

You could make another excuse, which is probably what some of you feel like you want to do right now. You want to make another excuse to cover up the excuse that I just exposed. If you feel like you want to make an excuse just say, "Look at what I'm doing." Just notice it for yourself.

# STRUGGLING TO SUCCESS

Becoming successful is a personal journey, as you read earlier. It's personal and individual to each one of us. For every one of us, this journey is a little bit different.

I have watched thousands of people over the years of my career all take a different journey, and it's personal to them. It means a great deal to them and to me. I have such respect and gratitude for being able to be a guide for those people who allow me to be a guide. I don't take that lightly.

I had to open myself up to let somebody guide me, and then I had to do something that was very important. My mentor put it to me this way. He said, "David, would you shut up and just listen for once?"

Because every time my mentor would say something to me, I would shoot my mouth off in some way, shape, or form to make an excuse as to why I couldn't do something or say, "What's going to happen if I do this?" He would say, "You need to stop and listen."

I remember learning that in other countries and throughout history, when a person got a mentor, there was a tremendous amount of respect for that individual. The mentee would do whatever the mentor asked them to do.

That was the deal when I worked with Bob. He said, "You're going to do what I tell you to do or I'm not going to work with you." I said, "Okay, I get that." I respect him tremendously and still do.

It seems like today I am watching people go to coaches and mentors, who are very good, but they do not have the proper respect for the people they have chosen to guide them. They have absolutely none whatsoever. The mentor or coach says, "You need to do this or that," and they don't do it.

When people who have come to me behave that way, I say, "Then I don't want to work with you either. I'm not here for your entertainment." People come to me because they know that they're going to get results. They come to me when they're ready to change.

You have to ask yourself a question. Why would you go to someone who has not demonstrated by results that they have done what it is that you want to do?

I see it all the time and I know other people see it all the time. People go to a seminar and observe somebody who has demonstrated that they have the results. Then that person will hire a coach inside the seminar who obviously doesn't have the results.

You'll ask them, "Why did you do that?" They say, "I resonate more with that person." Of course, they resonate more with that person. They're on the same damn level as you are. They're broke and so are you.

I didn't necessarily resonate with my mentor. I believed in what he said and I knew he had a different result. I wasn't looking for a love relationship. I was looking for someone that could challenge me and help me see what I could not see. That's what I want to do for you in this book.

I'm not your friend. I'm going to tell you that right now. I will be, however, the best friend that you've ever had. If I come into this relationship with you being your friend and we're all buddy-buddy, then I can't help you very much. I really can't.

There has to be a relationship between you and me where there is a certain degree of respect on both parts. I respect what you're going through and how difficult the change is, but I'm also very demanding in what it is that you do change. You won't read in this book that it's all good, because it isn't.

I will tell you that I believe I'm bringing you the best information that's out there, bar none. My concern is not whether you like me. Other people out there are scared to death that you won't like them. I don't care if you don't like me. It doesn't matter to me. I'm not here for you to like.

I'm here because I made a promise to God that I would help as many people change as I could while he allowed me to stay in this body. That was my promise when I had my near-death experience. I intend to keep that promise.

Part of that promise was not, "Only if people like me." No, it doesn't matter if you like me. What matters is if you are going to get a result.

I can guarantee you that, if you do exactly what this book instructs you to do, your life will never be the same again. You will get a result, and you will get the most amazing result. Do you want to know something else? You'll also have freedom.

I don't want people to work with me forever. If they work with me forever, they'll become dependent on me. That's not the idea. The idea is that I teach you something so that you can be free and then you go teach it to someone else. That's the miracle of money.

The miracle of money is getting that miracle into your life. It's been a miracle in my life and in the lives of countless people I've worked with. Now I want to get it into your life. In order to do that, you must overcome the resistance that's holding you back. You must stop making excuses. Saying that you don't have the money is just your subconscious mind creating an excuse. It's a ridiculous statement.

You are moving in the direction of how to reevaluate where you are, who you are, and what money is, as you've never seen before. This must be done in order create a new belief system that will allow you to get a new result.

If I say "instantly," I want you to know that my saying that means that it's possible for you. I would never give anybody information that they couldn't apply and get a result immediately. I just wouldn't do it. How long is it going to take you to apply it? I can't answer that because I'm not you.

I do know this. It doesn't matter what your need is. I know you can do it. How do I know you can do it? It's because I taught this to my oldest daughter's boyfriend when he was 18 years old, and he started building a million-dollar business. Was he a smart kid? Yes, but I don't think he was smarter than any other kid there was. I think he had a good work ethic. If he had any advantage over most of the kids at that age, I would say that he had a better work ethic.

I gave him the same idea at 18 years old. He was 18 years old, and this kid had more money than people that were 40. I am not kidding. It was because he did exactly what it is that I told him to do. I can give it to somebody who is 14 years old or 80 years old. It doesn't matter how old you are. You can do this, and you can apply it in your life.

Don't say, "I haven't started a business yet." It doesn't matter. I hadn't started a business either. I was driving a forklift, and I was in the back of a truck loading potato chips on a pallet. I worked for Kehe Food Distributors in Lisle, Illinois. Go look it up if you don't believe me. That's where I was, and I was miserable.

Then my life changed like night and day, and I was so blown away by how it changed that I had to find out what had happened. What changed? To put it simply, I started to evaluate things in a completely differently way than I ever had before. That allowed me to change my belief system. That allowed an instantaneous change in my result. That's what's about to happen for you.

There are real systematic things to do that will allow you to experience the miracle of money I your life. I think that is why you decided to read this book, not just to learn something intellectually but also to actually say, "Not only did I change on the inside, but I changed this. Now I've actually got the money that David said I would have."

Think about this for a second. Do you remember when I said when the excuse is perfect, it's perfect for each one of us? For 27 years, I made excuses that kept me exactly where I was. Do you know what the predominant thought in my mind was? It was, "Why is this happening to me?"

When I had my near-death experience, I changed the question a little bit. My question became, "Why can't I get myself to do what I know that I should be doing?" Do you know why I couldn't? It was because I was making excuses from morning to night. That's why.

When you stop making excuses and say, "I'm going to do this, and I'm going to focus on it. I'm going to do exactly what David says, and I'm going to let that be the judge."

A number of years ago when I worked with Alexandria Brown and watched her income skyrocket as a result of what it is that I taught her, she was so excited about the information that she called me up one day and said, "I would really like for us to do something together because we work so well together. We see eye-to-eye on this, and I had such an amazing experience in my life. Let's create something."

Because of change, because of what I gave her, because of how she put it in her life, we had one of those magic moments. You know what I mean. We had loosely talked about doing this for quite some time. Then we experienced one of those magic moments when everything comes together. This was one of those moments. A gift given became a gift received.

When you get a gift, turn around, and give it to someone else. Give it to someone else who needs it. It allows you to be a blessing. Just pass the blessing on because you're going to realize that it comes back to you. Blessings come back. Whatever you put out is going to come back.

## THE FOUR STEPS TO CASH ON YOUR JOURNEY TO ABUNDANCE

1. Know the difference between need and want.

2. Understand why you need that money.

3. The opportunity to bring money into your life is around your right now.

4. When you see the opportunity, act on it.


REMEMBER THE STEPS and TAKE THEM!

# MESSAGE FROM DAVID

I want to personally thank you for making the decision to significantly up-level your life and for purchasing my eBook!

I'm delighted to give you private access to 3 powerful bonuses (worth over $300!) not available anywhere on our website!

### Check the link to access your
# <u>Manifest Your Millions Within</u>
### eBook Series Gifts.
**(http://www.davidneagle.com/transform/kindlebook)**

I encourage you to download these **3 bonuses**

today and implement what you learn. Remember,

## "Through decision and action, anything

## is possible!"

-David Neagle

****************

## MORE KINDLE BOOKS FROM DAVID NEAGLE

When you're finished reading this book, download
the other volumes of the Manifest Your Millions
Within series by David Neagle available on
Amazon Kindle.

## The Mental Money Game
(http://www.amazon.com/Mental-Manifest-
Millions-Within-ebook/dp/B0081IOOL4)

## The Neagle Code
(http://www.amazon.com/Neagle-Manifest-
Millions-Within-ebook/dp/B0081KQ2AI)

## Mastering the Massive Cash Injection
(http://www.amazon.com/Mastering-Injection-
Manifest-Millions-ebook/dp/B0081KQ1JK)

## The 7 Mental Money Secrets of
## Millionaire Entrepreneurs
(http://www.amazon.com/Millionaire-
Entrepreneurs-Manifest-Millions-
ebook/dp/B0081IOOGY)

# ABOUT THE AUTHOR

In September of 1989, what was supposed to be a rare relaxing day with family cruising down the Illinois River in a roomy boat, quickly turned into a nightmare:

David Neagle was pulled deep into the gates of a dam that shredded his flesh, broke his back, and nearly drowned him. No one expected him to survive the accident, and rescue workers even told his family he was already dead. (Entire boats had been sucked into this same dam, without survivors.)

What happened instead is that David, a high-school dropout & dock worker, awakened to the potential previously untapped within him. He made a decision that day to begin the journey responsible for changing his entire life, and now the lives of thousands of others.

David Neagle, Master Success & Wealth Consciousness Mentor, knows how to help you achieve whatever dream your heart desires - no matter where you're starting from.

After his brush with death, David began to study his own potential. In the 12 months following his accident ~ despite being unable to walk for more than a month ~ he tripled his income! By

December of 2000, David had expanded to become an executive corporate manager, a stock investor, and a business owner!

Over the years, David continually sought new mentors with each new level of success he attained. He began to study every great person in history Ö but it wasn't until David began studying "The Science of Getting Rich", by Wallace D. Wattles, that he fully understood the transformation he'd undergone. Wattles' book uncovered the exact change in David's thinking and in his attitude that had gotten the ball rolling; to create his unstoppable success.

*"There is nothing more important in my life ~ or in my business ~ than my own personal growth as a human being. Truly, nothing is more important to me than shedding any piece of dysfunction that would hinder me from becoming the fullest representation of Spirit's great intention for me. Nothing."* ~ David Neagle

Today, David Neagle is the President of Life is Now, Inc., a multimillion dollar global coaching practice dedicated to teaching entrepreneurs, coaches, speakers, and service providers how to use the power of Universal Law to rapidly create quantum leaps in both business and personal arenas.

Forever an avid student, David's core mission is to bring expanded awareness & higher consciousness to as many people as possible, and to find greater ways of helping entrepreneurs to create massive cash injections more rapidly, so they can lead their greatest possible lives and serve the greatest number of people.

One of the ways he's best known for doing so, is via live, in-person events. David also privately mentors his own private VIP clients to host their own transformational live events, designed to generate in excess of 7-figures in under 4 days, and simultaneously provide the opportunity for those in attendance to up-level, implement the latest proven business growth strategies & step into community with other like-minded entrepreneurs!

Made in the USA
San Bernardino, CA
03 February 2016